Healthy Living for Women

IT'S MORE THAN MEETS THE MIND

Indie F. Jones, M.D.

www.mindfulhealth4women.com

Healthy Living for Women/Indie F, Jones, M.D. —1st ed.
ISBN 978-1722115685

Contents

PREFACE

Have you ever found yourself thinking, "Something has to give"? You are under undue stress at home and at the office. You can't figure out how you have gained 20 pounds in the last six months. The headaches, hot flashes, and fatigue are off the chart! You don't know how you are going to come up with your son's tuition, and you suspect your husband is cheating. Where do you begin? Where are the solutions? I suggest that everything will come into alignment when you begin to take care of yourself. This simple bit of advice may seem illusive to you at first. The real answers to the challenges that you face appear outside of yourself but come from within. As women, we tend to operate on autopilot. The job gets done but at what cost to our mental, physical, and spiritual health? When you become consciously aware of your thoughts, feelings, and emotions while keeping each in perspective, you will begin to make conscious decisions about your life that are beneficial to your overall well-being. You will become the author of the next chapter of your life. If you are in a major transition, you will harness the strength to endure while embracing your current situation with "presence." Let's begin your journey—where you will dig deep and welcome the knowledge of your true self, as uncomfortable as the process might be. This is where true spiritual growth begins.

INTRODUCTION

I deal with illness and death more often than the average person. As a doctor of internal medicine, my profession and the people I interact with have taught me a truth not everyone understands: Western medicine does not appreciate the full extent of the mind-body connection. Our minds play a key role in what happens to our bodies. Time after time, I've watched a patient's mindset promote the physical healing process. I have personally witnessed many a fighting spirit keep a patient alive much longer than any medical statistic would predict. The mind, body, and spirit—oh, how intricately connected and underappreciated. There are the times when your heart races, and you are aware of the emotion triggering it. It may be seeing your secret crush walk by, feeling anxiety before a speaking engagement, or anticipating unfavorable news. The emotions associated with the grieving process can manifest themselves in physical symptoms. I recall when I lost my father while in medical school to a rare disease that took his life abruptly. The morning of the funeral, I woke up with a crick in my neck that I attributed to sleeping in a bad position. That pain stayed in my neck for months, and it took a while for me to make the connection to my grieving process. Let's not forget about the "broken heart syndrome." A large surge of stress hormones triggered by emotions can literally mimic a heart attack and reduce the strength of the pumping action. My purpose for this writing is to highlight the overlooked connection of our minds to our state of health and to give you some practical tools to take charge of your own mind-body connection. Over the last several years, I have done some personal work to understand myself better, my fears, and my natural tendencies, including the ones that don't serve me well. It's not always a joyride. It means I should be realistic about what causes my emotions, even when I don't have them under control. We want to be careful to not rush into a situation that was not well thought-out and could prove harmful to our mental health. I reference my 22-year marriage that I entered into even when my higher-thinking brain had doubts. The woman I am now would have made different decisions— starting with being more in tune to "that still small voice." But I don't beat myself up over past decisions. Neither should you. We are all a work-in-progress. Each of us is fearfully and wonderfully made. I also believe we are formed in the image of a spiritual source of comfort, which for me is God. We suffer when we don't live as unique and multidimensional beings. It is my desire that, as you read, you will find out more about your uniqueness. Beyond that, I hope to help you see how the layers of your life are affected by the emotions you experience every day and how this can impact your health. My goal for you as you read these pages is to grasp peace, control in key areas of your life, and find joy in the process.

As a female doctor, I have a unique perspective on how to keep everything in balance on the path to true happiness. Because of what I have seen and personally experienced over the years, I am convinced that a proper mindset unlocks vast amounts of power we can apply to our individual lives. There are plenty of distractions in life that can put you in a haze or mental fog. Some people suffer from racing thoughts and a great deal of "mind chatter and clutter." As women, we are typically gifted at being able to multitask. Ultimately, there are times when we need more focus and tunnel vision for the mental task at hand. We can view our brains as the hard drive and our mind as the operating system. If the brain is somehow damaged by trauma, toxins, or poor nutrition, our minds and bodies are negatively affected. It's akin to getting a virus on your computer (brain), which then needs to be debugged. It's a well-known fact that we are influenced by the things that we are routinely exposed to. We take in information through our five senses, but are not consciously aware of the subliminal messages that go unfiltered via television and social media. The daily news is not short on tragedies, including crimes such as murder being committed every day. I am selective about what shows I watch because I try to protect myself from feeling sad or offended, when possible. It's not that I live in a bubble. I just know that I have choices, and so do you.

These choices that I make help me think more clearly, reason, and make good choices for my life. There is an entire field of medicine dedicated to mental health, which covers areas including depression and anxiety, as well as psychological conditions that affect our mood, personality, and behavior. I mention this only to stress how important one's mental health is. As it pertains to the spiritual and physical, it all starts with the mind. The well-known serenity prayer is a reminder of the power that we have within that creates our reality. When you know what you can change, you can seek the courage through prayer to take the necessary steps to change. Courage is acting despite the presence of apprehension and doubt.

This brings me to the topic of mindfulness. It is the nonjudgmental focus of your attention on the thoughts and emotions (sensations) that are present in the moment. By engaging in activities that promote mindfulness (meditation, nature walks, and other trainings), you reduce your risk of depression and anxiety. Mindfulness programs have also helped people with drug addiction. When you find yourself ruminating on the past or stressing over the future, it is important to consciously bring yourself back to the present. Working with a therapist or life coach can be beneficial.

CHAPTER 1

Your Secret Thoughts

The starting point with nurturing your mental and spiritual health is to discuss something that we all have or experience every day, hundreds to thousands of times a day: our thoughts. Our thoughts happen automatically. When we examine the history of our society and humankind, we were built to naturally have negative thoughts and be in the survival mode as we sought the necessities of life such as food, clothing, and shelter, while at the same time trying to avoid danger. I want to encourage you, however, to not place judgment on your negative thoughts. It is our thoughts that trigger emotions, which can turn into moods and mental states of being. It is not your job to try and erase negative thoughts. This may come as a surprise to you. I do believe in the role of positive thinking, but placing too much emphasis on the fact that you are having a negative thought will not be helpful. Let's do a brief exercise to show that this is futile. Pause after each of the following incomplete phrases and complete them either in your mind or out loud:

1. You can't teach an old dog _____.
2. What goes around _____ .
3. It's raining cats and _____ .

Now, I will venture to say that you got 100% on our little pop quiz. Even if you have not heard or used any of these phrases in a while, you remember them. You could not control having the missing words pop into your head. It's the same with negative thoughts. The question is whether you believe them. When it comes to negative self-talk, are you attached to the thoughts? Attachment gets in the way of your ability to act on the goals and aspirations that you have for your life. We can't control the random thoughts that occur throughout the day simply because of our brain's ability to remember. Neuroscience teaches us, however, that new thoughts are superimposed upon the old ones. In this fashion, the more positive thoughts that you begin to have will translate into beliefs that serve your life well. The old thoughts still pop up from time to time, but they don't have as much power as they used to.

But where do these old thoughts or beliefs come from? From the moment you came into this world, you were programmed and conditioned to think and behave a certain way. The way you are trained is dictated by the part of the world and the culture into which you were born. This includes the language you speak and religion you practice, as well as the social norms and mores. When you don't think or behave in alignment with the commonly accepted behavior, you begin to pass judgment on yourself and become your worst enemy. Fear begins to rule and reign. Negative thinking is the currency of fear, as you spend time dwelling on the past and punishing yourself for past mistakes. This handicaps your ability to live the best life that you can by affecting the quality of your overall health. Everything starts with the mind, including the decisions of what to meditate on, what you consume, and how you expend your energy. There are many techniques that can be used to help you avoid getting attached to negative thoughts. I think that it is normal to occasionally talk to yourself. For example, when I have a negative thought that this book will not be well received, I tell myself that it does not matter. My goal is to get the message out about how these concepts have tremendously helped me over the last several years and, if it can help just one woman, it will be well worth it. Also, I have been enjoyed the process and have continued to grow by it. You see, I did not focus on whether the thought was true or not. That is a waste of my time. Had I become attached to the thought, anxiety undoubtedly would have risen and controlled my actions; I would have stopped typing. In preparation for designing your health and wellness plan, let's try an exercise that can help. Write down a negative thought that keeps cropping up when you start setting your goals. Next, write the reason that your goal is vitally important to your life, irrespective of the thought. You may want to use separate pieces of paper and then tear up the negative thought. It may resurface, but you will begin to acknowledge its presence--and act in a positive fashion despite it. If you see that you are attached to the thought because it contains an element of truth, think about what you can do to set yourself up for success. For example, if you want to do a marathon in the next six months, your negative thought might be that you are overweight, de-conditioned, and in no way capable. I would think that the first two descriptions of your current state may be true. The last one, on capability, is a relative truth. It may be true as it relates to your current state, but won't be for very long once you get into a weight-loss program and hire a running coach.

Even though we have spontaneous thoughts through-out the day, we often repress the not-so-pleasant ones be-cause of the emotions that they elicit. What effect does repression have on your health? It is a defense mecha-nism against anxiety, one of the negative emotions that will be discussed in Chapter 2. Suppressing emotions can have major negative effects on your mental and physical health. This includes problems with the GI system such as irritable bowel syndrome, as well as increased levels of the stress hormone cortisol, leading to unwanted weight gain.

Emotions, Moods, Mindsets

Our emotions need to be acknowledged and managed because of the effects they can have on our health. I have learned in my own life that emotions are not the enemy. My life experiences have helped me realize that it's how we process and manage these emotions that makes a difference. That's hard to do because many times we don't want to be aware of the emotions that we would feel if we were to "tap in." That may be because some of our emotions make us feel like victims when life's circumstances, or even our own choices, create feelings that dominate us. Emotions can cause us to act in ways we later regret or that can cause shame. What's frustrating is that we keep repeating the process because these actions become habits. These habits can grow into the routines that grind on our souls. Sometimes, we just want to ignore what we are feeling.

Changing emotions affect even the simplest decisions. Sometimes, I may not be in the mood to do a Zumba class but push myself to go. The reward is another set of emotions created by the rush of the happy hormones or endorphins afterward. Translation? I didn't feel like it, did it anyway, and felt better when it was over. Emotional decisions can also have longer-lasting consequences. My life is an example here. Fear kept me in a very unhealthy marriage relationship for nearly 22 years! Reality for me means that my emotions cause me to try to understand what happens to me and why. One core truth is that just because I seek answers, I may not necessarily find them immediately, or at all. I'm comfortable with that now. I want you to look at your own emotions and see how they can become a barrier to good health and well-being.

A common pattern of unconscious behavior with negative health implications is emotional eating. It undoubtedly will result in unwanted pounds and feelings of guilt that lead to more emotional eating, thereby a repetition of the cycle. Let's discuss some ways that you can break the cycle.

It's time to reflect. You will need to have access to a full-length mirror and privacy to do this exercise. A perfect time would be immediately after you get out of the shower, when you are not in a rush to get to work or leave the house. I want you to dry off and then stand in front of the mirror. The goal is to begin to understand the mind-body connection as it relates to your eating patterns. It is not intended to be a "beat myself up for being overweight session." I want you to start with your eyes, the window to the soul. Ask yourself what the predominant emotion is that you are feeling. Are you sad, angry, fearful, happy? You may feel neutral. Take several deep breaths and tune into any sensation that you have in your body. This will help you identify the emotion. Now, look at your shoulders and note the degree of tension. Are they stiff or relaxed? Now the tough part. Look at your overall contour and note your curves, bulges, and genetically bountiful assets. What emotions arise? Are they the same as when you first looked in your eyes? Are your emotions shifting, intensifying, or remaining the same? Are you judging or feeling sorry for yourself? Take at least five minutes to describe what you are experiencing by writing in your journal.

For the next part of the exercise (you may dress first), I want you to describe any story that you may have as it relates to any negative emotions experienced when looking at yourself in the mirror. For example, you may have a story that your excess weight comes with age or that you don't have time to exercise and prepare healthy meals. If you feel stuck or helpless about your weight, it is important to turn any story on its head and figure out the psychological block that is preventing you from addressing what needs to change.

I know that I am very guilty of stress eating, as well as succumbing to the cravings and impulsive eating that we as women typically get every month. My story during those times of excess consumption is that I can't control it because it's my hormones' fault.

As you reflect, you will know whether emotional eating is a major problem. What will need to be practiced is "unlinking." You want to unlink food consumption from emotions, including something as simple as boredom. The first step to unlink is to start your food journal. One thing that most of us have easy access to is our cell phone, which can also be used to log and track what you are eating. Next, commit to not putting anything in your mouth for the next 72 hours without first documenting your mental state. If you are eating a minimal three meals per day, start with breakfast. You will dial in to your predominant emotion once you have decided to eat and then jot down the emotion (you may want to document why you feel a certain way). Next, set your stopwatch for five minutes and then begin to eat your meal. Take your time chewing and enjoying the food. I am not concerned about whether the food is healthy or not at this point. When the stopwatch sounds, stop eating and reset for another five minutes, but refrain from eating during this time. You can check your email or do something else to pass the time. Now, if you have finished the meal in the first five minutes, wait an additional twenty to determine if you are full. I suppose you would not be finished that fast unless it was a small snack. When the timer goes off the second time, continue to eat slowly and then repeat the exercise until you sense you are already full or the food has been completely consumed. At this point, I want you to assess if you are satisfied. Hopefully, this will be what you strive for as opposed to feeling stuffed or still hungry. If you still feel hungry, wait a total of thirty minutes from the time that you started eating to see if the perception of hunger is still there. Now, take note of the predominant emotion that you feel after the meal or snack is completely consumed. Research has shown that the hormone that signals satiety to our brains (leptin) is often elevated but not being perceived by our brains as it should be. Because of this, you are more inclined to overeat. This means that your brain will need some re-wiring. Next, document what you ate and classify if it falls in the category of comfort food (high carbohydrate or sugar content). This category is what becomes addictive to our brains because of how the food makes us feel. Food has essentially become a drug.

At the end of each day for the next three, determine what negative emotions may have contributed to what you ate, how frequently, and how much. There are plenty of practical methods for losing weight when it comes to what you eat and how often, such as six small meals every 3–4 hours. Before you can determine the technical aspects of how to make these adjustments, it is more important to process these negative emotions. It's time to get to the source of the emotions and not try to suppress them. Addressing the issues that cause frequent negative emotions instead of medicating with food is key. Don't judge the emotions; rather, make room for them and work on a holistic approach to address the distressing issues.

Below, you can see the overlapping nature of your mind, body, and spirit. No individual component functions independently of the others.

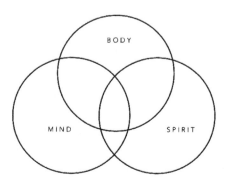

Let's look more closely at the mind/body/spirit connection by examining the following flow diagram:

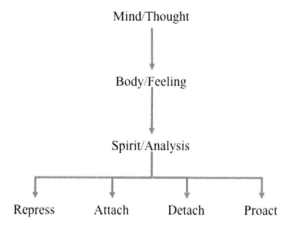

The many thoughts we have trigger sensations or emotions that we often don't know how to handle. These physical responses are very much a product of our personality, which was shaped at a very young age, coupled with our life experiences. Two individuals can have similar tragedies occur in their lives yet have a very different processing of the emotions generated by the memories, resulting in different responses (action vs. inaction).

Let's take the example of one of my childhood memories that when processed a certain way led to the delay in my dream of being a doctor. As I contemplated my path in life at age 19, I made the decision that I was going to focus more on getting married than pursuing my education. I was finishing college, but marriage was the next step at age 22. I knew that, with all my heart, I wanted and needed to be a doctor, but I received many messages throughout my childhood that I could not. My loving mother and siblings had concerns that I would not do the things that I needed to do to become a doctor once I said, "I do," and they were right. When the subject was brought up, the negative tapes were re-wound and the words were loud and clear in my head. I recall taking an exam in high school that was designed to tell you what you should and could pursue in life. Apparently, my creative brain was very active that day because, weeks later, the results were that medicine was far from my capabilities and that I was better suited for business and the arts. I was devastated, because my personality is such that I internalize the opinions of others. I have grown in this area over the years however; as you can see, but let's go through the diagram with my experience. I want you to learn how you can make the necessary shifts in your response to those events that keep you stuck in life. First, I had the memory of the negative feedback from that awful exam. The sensation in my body each time I had this memory and other similar experiences was a sinking feeling in my abdomen, which equated to self-doubt and general low self-esteem. My spirit analyzed the situation, and I then became attached to the false message that was conveyed. I recall that one of my classmates received results indicating she could be anything that she wanted to be, and I can vividly recall her grinning from ear to ear while I sank in my chair feeling despair and that I didn't even belong in that elite all-girls Catholic high school that my mother felt was going to give me the best education. The attachment to these stories, created from my emotional response to the memories, resulted in a self-fulfilling prophecy for a season. I stopped studying, and I stopped trying. Of course, the results were not favorable, and the cycle would continue with self-defeating behaviors, which would give me the very dreaded results that I did not want. I unwittingly watered the seeds that were planted in my heart and let them sprout and cloud my judgment. What area in your life has become a negative self-fulfilling prophecy? Write down the thought, your emotional reaction, your spiritual evaluation, and commit to executing a proactive solution. You see, I became proactive many years later after I took a few small steps, even though I was still doubting.

Nonetheless, the force of God was moving despite the poor choices that I made and the inaction that delayed things. God blessed me amid my confusion and perpetual looking for love and acceptance outside of myself. This was the missing piece: self-love. We all have heard about being, "sick and tired of being sick and tired." Well, I had my epiphany just a few years ago, after my divorce. I had to do the work and did work with a life coach after having gone through some professional counseling with a pastor as well as a psychologist. I learned that it was okay to think about my own needs. This was counterintuitive for me, of course. My whole life had been committed to looking for answers outside of myself instead of from within. From the pastor to the coach, I was encouraged to seek my own truth. I would still rely on the fundamental truths that I had been taught by my mother and religious teachers, but they would serve as a framework to evaluate my personal life experience. I was not going to get daily instructions from an audible voice or by any future-telling mechanism. I had to figure things out for myself as I began to live a new life with a new sense of freedom and control. So, you can see my method of learning to "detach" from what had me "attached" and enslaved.

The healthiest response that you can have to painful memories or negative thought patterns is to be aware of them, not attach (detach when necessary), not repress, but acknowledge and address. This is the proactive arm of the diagram. I was inspired by a mother whose child I cared for in my home daycare that I had when my now

23-year-old son was still in diapers. At the time, she was in her OB-GYN residency. She was married and had six children! When discussing her journey, she shared that any time someone told her that she could not do something, it ignited something in her to prove them wrong! She certainly did not internalize any negative input.

Emotions can have a devastating effect on your physical health when warning signs are not addressed. I have seen both the young and old female patient ignore that new lump in their breast. The fear of cancer is suppressed, and the obvious concern does not get addressed in a timely fashion. There is a level of denial, which has grave consequences. There was an attachment to fear instead of an acknowledgement of it, and appropriate action. Talk about your fears and concerns and elicit the help of those who love you to support you through the process of addressing new health concerns. As you assess your overall health, go through the flow diagram to see how much your thoughts and emotions are working against you because of your processing skills. We will go into more detail as we look at various emotions that we all experience.

Depression

As women, most of us have this natural tendency to cater to everyone else's needs but our own. However, self-care is so very important and under-rated. There is this psychological guilt trip that we place on ourselves, which over time can affect our mental and physical health to the point that we become incapacitated. I recently evaluated a young lady in the emergency department who was suffering from depression and had come to check herself into the mental-health facility. She apparently had turned her young children over to foster care, as she was at her wit's end. I did not get her whole story as I was only evaluating her for a few chronic medical conditions. The sad commentary is that depression had overwhelmed her. She was anemic, had hypertension, and was significantly overweight as well. Her poor mental health was undoubtedly affecting her physical health and her ability to take care of her offspring. I asked myself, "Why wasn't she able to deal with life's stressors in a healthy fashion? What were those obstacles that she perceived as insurmountable?" All I could do was wonder. From a medical perspective, there is a real disease process or chemical imbalance called clinical depression. Some suffer from bipolar disorder with major mood swings. It is hard to seek help when you are feeling so down and despondent. That's why it is important for everyone to have someone who can be trusted, is non-judgmental, and can lend a listening ear. Clinical depression, however, is diagnosed by a medical professional based on certain criteria. You may require medication to boost the level of the happy hormones in your brain. If you feel that you are suffering from depression, it is key to discuss this with your primary-care physician. On the other hand, there is something called situational depression. As the name implies, it happens when a situation occurs, such as losing a loved one. Everyone grieves in their own way. The reality is that the sad feelings of grief should not be avoided but rather allowed to run their course. That is, practice feeling the emotions all the way through. Anger is certainly a part of the process. Allow yourself to cry and find healthy ways of releasing the frustration. When my dear sister Chris died suddenly from an unknown cause, there were days that I forced myself to go to the gym and exercise. I didn't experience the full euphoria that I normally do, but it was a means to cope and avoid getting stuck in a rut. I didn't allow my sadness to become an obstacle to maintaining my physical health. I had to make a conscious decision to keep up my routine even if I did not feel like it. Had I not, no doubt I would have started putting on excess pounds from inactivity. That is why I recommend making a routine assessment of your level of energy and see if there is a correlation to an emotion. I must say that it would have been perfectly fine for me to stay at home in bed those days, but I decided to work through the pain. I didn't want to have a complicated grief reaction. If there is any doubt about a grieving process that you are going through, please seek professional help! For some, journaling is therapeutic. It can be helpful with any situation that makes you sad or depressed. As women, we have various hormone fluctuations every month. You may suffer from PMS. There is another condition called premenstrual dysphoric disorder. Several years ago, I suffered from this. I would become depressed and feel on edge for half of the month. I would not feel relief until the onset of menstrual flow. If you see a pattern of depression like this, taking an antidepressant for two weeks out of the month has proven to be helpful. There are other things that can be done to help minimize the symptoms, such as healthy nutrition, exercise, and proper rest. You should have some basic bloodwork checked, including your vitamin D level, hemoglobin/iron, and thyroid function. These simple blood tests can reveal deficiencies that can contribute to the symptoms of depression. If you are perimenopausal, this presents a unique set of challenges. This phase of our womanhood can last for as long as ten years prior to menopause, which is marked by 12 consecutive months of no menstrual flow. You will have irregular periods and more than likely suffer from hot flashes. Your risk of depression rises as well. You will need to discuss the risks and benefits of supplemental estrogen to help alleviate the hot flashes and vaginal dryness with your gynecologist. Bottom line, speak to your primary care doctor or gynecologist to determine a proper diagnosis and treatment plan.

Anxiety

Anxiety is an emotion that we all experience from time to time. An anxiety disorder, however, is a predominating state of being that can be characterized by symptoms, such as constant worry, restlessness, and difficulty sleeping at night. If you feel anxious often, it is time to seek an evaluation from a medical professional, such as your primary-care doctor or psychiatrist. Anxiety is an emotion evoked by the contemplation of something in the future. It can be something that you know is supposed to happen or it may be one of those stories that we like to create. Anxiety and fear may elicit some of the same physical responses, but there is a distinction between these emotions. Fear is experienced when there is something tangible that causes it. A classic example is the bear in the woods. If you encounter one, your heart rate undoubtedly will increase as well as your breathing rate. Your palms will more than likely become sweaty and there will be increased blood flow to your leg muscles preparing you to run. This is a healthy natural response that is protective. Anxiety exists without a tangible danger in front of you and is never beneficial.

One thing that I know about myself is that I want instant answers and knowledge of the future as if I could look in a crystal ball for it! What I have had to learn to practice, however, is the art of staying present. All any one has is the present moment. We can and should make preparation for the future, set goals, and dream big! It's when we get stuck in the future that anxiety can arise and have adverse effects on our mental health. This can affect the secretion of hormones in the digestive tract and, in more severe cases, cause symptoms of irritable bowel syndrome, headaches, and elevated blood pressure that can lead to a stroke or heart attack. Meditation is a wonderful way to practice being present or staying in the moment. The nervous anticipation of the future, which comes with anxiety, will begin to diminish with time and practice. One thing to add to your meditation is visualization of the opposite thing that you are anxious about. Begin to train your brain to be just as elaborate, if not more, with the positive version of what you are anticipating. See it and experience it with your mind's eye. The truth is that sometimes you will bring about the very thing that you dread (Law of Attraction). On the other hand, when less-than-positive things happen despite our positive energy, it is not time to give up! Again, I am inspired by my patients in this area. My hero is a young lady in her 30s who was diagnosed and treated for one of the more challenging forms of breast cancer. She expressed to me that it was her mindset that got her through the not-so-pleasant treatments, and she is ready to help educate other young women going through similar experiences.

Loneliness

We have many catch phrases to describe the degree to which a person is inclined to be in the presence of others. On one end of the spectrum, you have the "loner" and, on the other is the "people person." An important distinction to be made is that the person who prefers to spend time alone is not lonely. Conversely, the extrovert can still feel lonely surrounded by those she loves. Lone-liness is that distressed feeling that you have when your social needs are not being met and you feel isolated. A startling statistic indicates that loneliness has become an epidemic in the US, with some 40% of adults report-ing feeling lonely. We have all had times in our lives when the feeling of loneliness comes to visit–uninvited. Sometimes, this unwelcome visitor stays a little too long, as can be felt when a long-term relationship comes to an end. Research also shows the negative effect that a per-sistently lonely feeling can have on a person. A few of the increased health risks are: accelerated aging process, increased blood pressure, personality disorders, psy-chosis, impaired cognitive ability, Alzheimer's dementia, depression, obesity, and cardiovascular disease (strokes and heart attacks).

When I reflect on the circumstances that bring many of my patients to the emergency department, I must ac-knowledge that this research is not all that surprising. You see, persistent feelings of loneliness can lead to poor self-regulation, which leads to poor health behaviors. I can examine my patient census to see who is psychologi-cally and physically dependent on chemical substances to feel normal. The admitting diagnosis could be drug overdose, alcohol-related cirrhosis, and failure to thrive from not eating, to name just a few. A lack of initiative to take care of your health is also a consequence of persis-tent lonely feelings.

If you find that loneliness is negatively impacting your health, a little work needs to be done to get to the root of your feeling disconnected. Do you generally enjoy being around people? There is a level of vulnerability that you will need to embrace to create a sense of connectedness with others. It takes some initiative. Often, our busy lives would have us fall off on communicating and spending time with those whom we love and care about. Make a list of five friends or family members you will reach out to over the next five weeks. Are you comfortable with your social skills? Be open to venturing out and exploring new experiences via local social groups or organized social events at your church or place of worship. Are you feeling disconnected from your spouse? Take some time to meditate and reflect on the reasons why, without having a judgmental attitude. Counseling may be of benefit to you discovering the barriers to your level of intimacy.

There is an important caveat to assessing your loneliness. That is, you should be comfortable in general with alone time. If you are single, does it make you so uncomfortable that you find yourself jumping in and out of dysfunctional relationships? It could be that you need time to learn more about yourself and to value and appreciate who you are, as well as who you want to become. The bottom line is that feeling lonely is just another emotion to learn to manage. The more you focus on loving and appreciating yourself, the better equipped you will be to have positive, meaningful relationships that don't define you but rather add to the experience of your happiness. You also don't want to trade loneliness with having toxic relationships. This will have the same, if not worse, effects on your health. How do you know that you are in such as relationship? Here is a non-exhaustive list of things that might suggest that you are:

1. You are afraid to have an opinion of your own for fear of ridicule.
2. You are always walking on eggshells to avoid a fight.
3. You feel like you are a child and need permission to do things.
4. There are acts of jealousy and/or threats.
5. You fear for your safety.
6. You feel that you can do no better or are unworthy.
7. Their happiness is dependent on you.
8. Constant drama.
9. You are always at fault.
10. Your gut tells you it is an unhealthy relationship.

So, what do you do if there is a resounding yes? It certainly depends on the circumstances and the odds that things can change. If it is your spouse, this can be very challenging, as you would want to bring in a professional third party to help work through things if he is willing to seek help. It is important that this third party is objective and professional, so that you avoid the drama triangle at all costs (covered in Chapter 5)! We all need that close friend or family member in whom we can confide, but it is best to not let them get in the mix or begin confronting your spouse in an attempt to "rescue you."

Frustration

We all experience frustration from time to time. It can be internal or external. Think of the person who suffers from road rage—hopefully you are not one of them! This person has a much lower frustration tolerance than the 2-year-old who is often heard saying "me do it" when attempting to dress herself properly again and again. This calm persistence and tolerance of failure somehow gets lost as we age. Let's look at what effects feelings of frustration can have on the body:

1. Decreased oxygen to the cells of the body due to shallow breathing or breath holding.
2. Decreased elimination of toxins from cells.
3. Increased hormones that raise your heart rate and increase your blood pressure.
4. Slowed digestion.

There are certain expectations that we have with any effort at making beneficial changes in our lives. When we don't get the results that we want, the frustration can become overwhelming and counterproductive. My personality is such that if I can't get something right, I will keep at it because I can't stand the feeling of defeat. You may be different and just give up because of the lack of satisfaction and gratification from your efforts. Practicing a healthy lifestyle by making good choices with your eating habits and routine exercise requires a conscious effort and plan. Sometimes, when life's monkey wrenches get thrown in, frustration sets in, and it's easy to resort back to your unhealthy ways.

It may be that you just need a fresh approach to your plans, as well as a critical analysis of ways that you may be sabotaging yourself. For example, if you are trying to maintain a healthy weight by going to the Zumba class three times a week but you see that you have gained 10 pounds since last year, this would definitely be discouraging. I have seen some very dedicated gym members who are at the gym participating in the various classes and working up a sweat. They are always there and are very committed, but their weight does not correspond to their efforts. I don't know how frustrated they may or may not feel. An educated guess tells me that, barring any medical condition such as an underactive thyroid, the problem is what they are eating. Also, your body gets used to the same routine, which is why it is important to change things up and challenge yourself.

Perseverance and an assessment of the need to changing your approach to your health and wellness are key to your success. Trying some one-on-one coaching can also help you discover the best tools for you to use in building your master plan.

When you start to feel frustration and the effects that it is having on your body (such as headaches and tension), begin to "pause, breath, clear, and look for the reveal." This four-step approach will reduce the negative effect that feelings of frustration have on your mind and body. Let's look at them one at a time.

Pausing involves the conscious decision to place what you are doing on a temporary hold. You are simply trying to regroup. Now take a few deep cleansing breaths. You are not getting the results that you are desirous of. Try to clear your mind of the thought process that seems to not be working and look for an innovative approach to be revealed. You may want to elicit the suggestion of someone who has more experience in the area or whom you admire and possibly see as a role model. Ask yourself if what you are trying to accomplish is realistic, controllable, and important. Of course, taking better care of yourself would get a resounding yes to all of these. It is a matter of what works for you based on your individual life circumstances that will dictate the details.

Unforgiveness and Resentment

"Father forgive them for they know not what they do." The principle of forgiveness is not just a religious construct. Psychologists around the world can undoubtedly recount thousands of counseling hours spent helping a client work through feelings of resentment and anger that comes with the inability to forgive. Forgiveness comes easier for some than others.

It is key to note that forgiveness does not in any way mean that you allow yourself to be used as someone's doormat, where their baggage is left at the doorstep of your heart and you are expected to be the concierge that doesn't get a tip! The thing about not forgiving is that it leads to resentment, which can eat at your soul. It affects every aspect of your health—mental, physical, and spiritual. The person you are doing a favor, when you are able to forgive, is yourself. Notice I said when you are ABLE. When you are in the raw of your pain and drama, it is not that easy. The forgiveness is not contingent on the person's willingness to say sorry or change. You make the decision if he or she has any place in your life or if ties need to be severed for the sake of your well-being. Forgiveness is a process that, if you are willing to WORK through, will reap innumerable benefits. When you can view every person as an ally perfectly designed to teach you something about yourself and life, that is when you become FREE AT LAST! I know that some wounds run deep. In the hospital setting, nurses are responsible for doing a thorough skin assessment on every patient that comes in. There are stages of wounds and wound healing. Sometimes, a wound nurse will do what's called a bedside debridement. This is where dead tissue is removed so that the blood flow can support the formation of new healthy tissue. Sometimes this tissue is foul smelling, and you may need antibiotics to take care of an underlying infection in the wound. I know that some of the things that you have experienced in life have been very foul and putrid. There is an active role that you must play in the healing process. If you mentally choose to look beyond the wound and look at your entire body, you will realize that you have not been destroyed. In the same manner, practice changing how you view betrayal and unthoughtful acts.

Think of at least three different scenarios of something either past or present that is an area of difficulty with forgiving someone. Describe the details of the scenarios: (find a quiet place with no distractions and please take your time):

1. What happened?
2. Did you play a role in perpetuating the situation?
3. What fears kept you from taking control?
4. What life lessons were learned?
5. If you are still in pain, what steps can you take to heal and move on.

One of the worst betrayals is that of an unfaithful spouse. Some couples can recover and build an even stronger bond, but this takes time and work. Healing can be hampered when there is minimization, blame, and ongoing deceit.

Whether or not you stay in the marriage, it is essential that you work on yourself. The most commonly affected area is your self-esteem. Adultery is a form of rejection and usually one that does not make much sense. The other person is neither better looking, smarter nor kinder than you. You may discover that there is a major character flaw, personality disorder, or traumatic childhood that is at the

root of things. Professional counseling is key. I recommend that you get the individual therapy that you need
regardless of your spouse's willingness to go as a couple.
You may have been completely abandoned and left with
a broken heart, dependent children, and no money, if
you are a stay-at-home mom. You will undoubtedly need
much love and support of family and friends during and
after a divorce.

How do you begin to feel good about yourself again?
When you are married, particularly at an early age, you
can lose yourself, but as time passes, we all change. Some
may not have the emotional maturity to weather life's
storms and grow together through these changes. Once
divorced, I realized that not only did I need time to find
myself and heal the brokenness, but I also developed a
burning desire to recreate myself. You, too, are like one
of God's most fascinating creations, the butterfly. There
are so many messages that it gives us. Like the butterfly,
you are changing. Just like the butterfly does with its external skeleton, you too can weather the external harsh
conditions that you face from time to time, including
the trauma of divorce. This is because of your ability to
adapt to the environment and climatic conditions. The
butterfly has four stages to its metamorphosis. Our four
stages can also be compared to the seasons. We change
mentally, physically, and spiritually. The change is inev-
itable. Beauty radiates from you throughout the process.

Take the next 10–15 minutes for some journaling. If
you are divorced, describe who you were in the following

five areas before marriage, during, and after (you can create a chart for comparison):

1. Level of self-esteem
2. Degree of ambition
3. Zest for life
4. Degree of spirituality
5. Ability to trust your own thinking and reasoning

What patterns do you see? Things may be very raw for you right now, and that is okay. This is intended to give you an idea of the areas that you can work on. What interests do you have time for, now that you are in your singleness? This is the perfect time to do you! It's actually very fun, too!

Guilt and Shame

If you are at all like me, you may find that the most difficult person to forgive is yourself. Guilt can eat at your spirit and subconsciously cause self-punishment. Constant feelings of guilt can increase the levels of the stress hormone cortisol as well as adrenaline. This increases your risk of diabetes, depression, and hypertension. How many times have you beaten yourself up over the poor choices that you have made in the past—especially those that deal with past relationships? "I should have known better," and, "How could I have been so stupid?" These are just a couple of common themes of negative self-talk. The more you put yourself down, the more time you spend spinning your wheels and going nowhere fast. I heard it once described like this: the reason that the rear-view mirror is so much smaller than the front windshield is that your future is much bigger and brighter than your past! You only need to glance at the rearview mirror from time to time to remind yourself where you are headed. Learn to have self-compassion. Many of the choices that you made were based on the limited information that you had at the time. In an abusive or toxic relationship, you may have seen some red flags that were ignored because you wanted to believe the false representative. The more we learn to value ourselves, the easier it is to learn from past mistakes and gain the strength to make drastic changes, set boundaries and, at times, sever ties. Does your inability to forgive yourself make you feel unworthy of happiness? Do you sabotage yourself by following a diet that consists mostly of nutritionally poor, high-calorie foods? Are you using sex, alcohol, or narcotics to self-medicate and numb the pain? The answer to these may be painful, but the introspection is needed to begin healing and growing. There is help for you. Let go of the shame and ask for it.

Also, it is important to not be shamed by others. Let your past be your past. There may be some behaviors that would fall in the category of immorality. You have changed. Your mindset and life are not the same. Take the power back from anyone who tries to hold your past over your head. You don't have to prove yourself to anyone when you know who you are today. You should keep these individuals who want to remind you of your past at arm's length. If it is a loved one, set boundaries for what you will allow yourself to be a recipient of.

Self-Doubt

Whatever your health and wellness goals are, you may be of the belief that YOU are not capable of achieving them. Research suggests that as children get older, self-doubt and self-judgment causes a steady decline in cognitive function. These feelings stem from the negative messages that are conveyed by adults, be it our well-intentioned parents or by those in authority, such as a teacher. Over time, self-doubt can lead to anxiety and depression and can be linked to chronic fatigue, high blood pressure, and increased complications of heart disease. If self-doubt is hindering you from taking care of yourself and achieving your dreams, it is time to work on being present. It's time to see your value to this world and begin walking with and in YOUR purpose. You see, you can find yourself walking very purposefully in the wrong direction! Taking the steps toward achieving better health equips you to fulfill your purpose. We know that perfection is impossible, but we certainly can strive toward optimization so that we can operate more efficiently. It's vitally important to not compare yourself to others and to be your authentic self. The gifts and talents that you have should not be hidden and taken to the grave with you!

I am often amazed at the strength of those with handicaps and amputees you hear about in the news and media. Instead of doubting their capabilities, they find a way to do the things that they love, and that the average able-bodied person wouldn't even dare to dream.

I am sure that it comes as no surprise that a fulfilling life will result in a sense of well-being. What dreams have you placed on hold or put in the impossible category that need to be revived? There were times that my deferred dream to become a physician was thought to be buried never to be resurrected. I explain later in the discussion of spiritual health how it took some time for me to be proactive in my self-actualization process. Take the next 20 minutes to start writing in your journal. Describe your dream life in the following areas:

1. Level of peace
2. Level of energy
3. Level of fitness
4. Ideal weight
4. Dream career
5. Dream home and location
6. Ideal relationships (God, partner, friends, or family)
7. Dream vacation
8. Level of wealth
9. Ideal manifestation of a talent or acquiring a new skill.

10. Ideal gift from you to society

Now, place the areas in order from most to least important. Take each one and analyze your faulty thinking that hinders you from creating a plan. Go down your list tackling one area at a time, devise your strategy, and watch how you begin to realize what you visualize. Being patient with yourself is key. In each area, you are in complete control. Be bold and act, even when the doubt is present. It can be in the passenger seat, but never let it take the wheel.

Next, I want you to take each letter of the word DOUBT and create a novel word that depicts your strongest attributes and qualities. For example:

D-etermined

O-ptimistic

U-nmoveable

B-old

T-alented

Describe in detail some examples that demonstrate these characteristics. Every time you get that feeling inside that halts your progress, chant your qualities like a cheerleader and feel the angst dissipate! Your confidence will build with each small success that you have. You will be like a tree planted by the water, yielding fruit in YOUR SEASON.

Stress

Unhealthy stress can weaken the immune system. It can also lead to overeating. We all have the normal stress that comes with living as we juggle wearing our various hats as mother, wife, daughter, friend, and CEO.

I just worked eight days in a row and feel mentally and physically drained. It usually takes me a day or two after such a long stretch to recuperate and regenerate. My profession involves critical thinking, which at times can be so intense that at the end of the day I feel as if I ran a marathon! At work, as I look up lab results, order more tests, and try to come up with the correct diagnosis and treatment plan, I'm required to be able to think on the fly as well as contemplatively, as I often do at home. So how do I do it? Proper rest is vitally important. I also enjoy pampering myself with massages as well as manicures and pedicures. Listening to soft jazz is another one of my favorite ways to unwind.

I began to appreciate the therapeutic effect of exercise six years ago when I began my journey toward weight loss and fitness. I lifted weights for thirty minutes with a trainer three times per week. I slowly lost about 25 pounds after a few months without even changing my eating habits. That came later. I guess you can call it my personal "Get up and move program." The key is to find what works for you. Resistance training, however, with weights or other objects, is important for women as we age. It is important for our bones and muscle mass. You won't bulk up! Become more active by doing what you enjoy and change it up from time to time. I'm a member of several hiking groups and love music and dancing (i.e., Zumba).

Let's now take a moment to tune in and see if you sense any tension in your body. How is your breathing? Do you typically take very shallow breaths? I presume that, at this moment, you are not aware of the breaths that you take from one second to the next. Slow, steady, deep breathing, however, has many health benefits. You are essentially enhancing oxygen exchange, which in turn helps every single cell in your body, improves circulation, and relaxes the smooth muscles in your blood vessels. This relaxation helps to lower your blood pressure. Everyone in my immediate family has been diagnosed with hypertension, so it made sense that I would be diagnosed as well, giving the family a 100% participation rate! I have two very vivid recollections of feeling my elevated blood pressure. The first time was when I was an intern and my youngest was three months old. You can imagine the stress that I was under with the very role of internship, being in a new town, and still breastfeeding an infant when I was not at the hospital. One day, while on rounds, I knew something was wrong because I was not only fatigued but had a pressurized feeling in my head. Something told me to have my blood pressure checked, and it was 170/100 (textbook normal is less than 120/80)! I was so disappointed that I had been ushered into the "high blood pressure club" due to my family's history and genetics. I was fortunate to have symptoms, given that so many people walk around with high blood pressure and no symptoms. This increases the risk of having a heart attack or stroke. Fast forward about eight years. I had that feeling again, and my pressure was back up. The top number was over 200 while I made my rounds at the hospital. I didn't feel like I was under any undue stress, which is why I did not understand why I got that same feeling like I had had when I was an intern. I had been able to manage my blood pressure with diet and exercise but now I was back on one pill. Knowing your body is so important. As I said, my MIND told me that something was wrong with my BODY! It is also vitally important to know your family's history to combat this silent killer. Stress can exacerbate your hypertension even with medications on board. What areas in your life seem to cause you the most heightened level of stress? Can you just make a conscious decision to "Let go and let God?" I made that decision recently with the stress of being a single parent raising a male child with ADHD. I found myself getting very upset and, at times, yelling at the top of my lungs, which is very uncharacteristic for me. Despite my love and concern over my child's future and desire for him to be successful, I had to realize that I cannot control another human being's behavior—not even my minor child, who came out of my womb! All I can do is set boundaries and set him up for success while holding him accountable for his actions. No matter how desirous I am for the

outcome of good grades and consistent upstanding behavior, I cannot control either.

Right now, I would like for you to list the top three
areas of stress that are negatively affecting your mental
and physical health. How will you choose to change your
mindset about the situation? You may want to try meditation. It's not that complicated. Just take a few minutes
a day to close off all external stimuli and practice deep
breathing. I have started re-training my brain by listening
to gospel music on Pandora in my car on my way to work.
I use this time to pray as well.

What can you do during your stressful work day to
relieve the pressure? Can you take even just five minutes
every so often to go to a quiet place to breathe deeply or
pray? What form of exercise will you engage in for at least
thirty minutes, three times a week? Write the answers
down. You will be amazed at the sense of relief now that
you have a strategic plan to combat the unhealthy reactions that you are having to what your mind perceives as
stress.

Apathy

To act on something, you must feel something about
it. The interesting thing about apathy is that it is the feeling of not feeling. One of my patients today was sadly
an example of apathy. She weighed over 300 pounds
and was in the hospital for back pain related to disc dis-

ease and her weight. It was the day of discharge and her nurse described the sad scene of the patient lying in bed and eating a big tub of ice cream while watching a show on TV about weighing over 600 pounds! She relayed that it sounded like her life. With apathy, there is an indifference and unresponsiveness to the messages that are being sent your way and an unconsciousness about your state of being. Sometimes, we convince ourselves that things can't change or that change is not important. We are under an illusion and there is a spell that needs to be broken.

Apathy overlaps with some of the other emotions that have been discussed, and it is important to get to the root of the problem.

I'm also reminded of my stroke patients. Some strokes can leave a patient in a state of neglect of one side of their body. Their brain must be retrained to hopefully regain the functions lost. At times, there may be a loss of sensation in certain parts of their body. This can also be seen with my diabetic patients who have the complication called neuropathy, which causes numbness and tingling. There is a damaging of the nerves from prolonged exposure to very high blood sugar levels that have become toxic.

What retraining of your brain needs to take place and what toxins have overtaken your mind and caused you to lose hope of what can and should change in your life? Is it the toxic relationships, negative thoughts about past hurts and pains, or feelings of unworthiness? It's time to press the reset button. Look inside and acknowledge what you truly feel. Look in the mirror and acknowledge what you truly see. Then, rest in these emotions and know that everything else is external and consequential of one life event affecting another.

I am confident that I have not even scratched the surface of the emotions and mindsets that can hinder optimal health and well-being. Hopefully, you can continue the process of introspection and remaining present while making room for your emotions and engaging in behaviors that will work for and not against you.

CHAPTER 3

Fallacies

Much of our challenge in maintaining a healthy balance in life and reducing unhealthy stress stems from our faulty belief systems. When you feel stuck in a rut with taking charge of your health and your life, it's time to take a critical look at four key areas of unrealistic expectations.

Control Fallacy

First, there is the fallacy of control. You can either believe that you can control everything or that you have no control at all. This is also known as internal control. You assume responsibility for both the pain and happiness of others. Now, that probably sounds ridiculous to you, but I would like for you to examine your relationships and see if your actions speak to this. If you are a mother, you can probably relate to the pain that is felt when you see your child hurting. You immediately want to fix whatever the problem is, and you may feel that you are letting your child down when you can't take the pain away. I've been there. You may even feel guilt and responsible. For example, with contemplating getting a divorce, many women will stay in an unhealthy relationship for the sake of the children without realizing that there may be more harm done by staying in the relationship. This is not an endorsement of divorce. The fact is that everyone, child or adult, can learn to heal and adapt to major life changes and tragedies that are part of life and living.

Another aspect of relationships is the reasonable expectation that if each one does his or her part, everything will flow in harmony. We get into trouble when we micromanage and don't allow the ones closest to us to walk in their own autonomy. If you have a perfectionist personality, no one is ever going to do things the proper way according to your standards. You will be disappointed every time. Your disappointment is usually not conveyed in the most constructive fashion, which in turn creates tension, frustration, and undue stress on the mind and body. If you find yourself attempting to have complete control, stop and ask yourself: "What is the worst thing that could happen if things don't go my way?" When you can acknowledge your inability to control others or have complete control over situational outcomes, the unnecessary weight of trying to do so should be easily released and you will begin to have peace.

The opposite extreme of this is a sense of helplessness or having no control at all. There is the idea that fate has something to do with the negative outcomes to the relationships and situations in your life. Now, we can spin "fate" in a positive light. I know that fate played a role in my life, with becoming a physician. However, it was not going to just happen for obvious reasons. I had to do something. I had to do a lot of things! I did my part and God did the rest for me.

Another aspect of feeling that you have no control, and that will keep you stuck, can stem from a lack of boundaries or assertiveness. Your fear of just saying "NO" will have you feeling that you can't change situations that you can. It is not so much what happens to you in life but rather how you respond. Back to relationships. It is never advisable that you give someone an ultimatum. I am not speaking so much about parenting, as this is a completely different dynamic. What about with your spouse? Can you instead operate in your own truth and let your actions speak louder than words? This is not a proposition to act out of spite. When you begin to take time for yourself and express what you are doing in the spirit of love, it speaks volumes. The husband and teenaged children will figure out what to do for dinner if you decide to start going to the gym after work three times a week. Maybe they will have your healthy plate ready for you when you do get home!

You can choose to not let your blood pressure be affected when your buttons are being pressed. Take the power away and feed your spirit by doing whatever it leads you to do in the moment, even if it means removing yourself from the situation. I hope you are getting the message that there is a great deal of power and strength that you have at your disposal. It is a matter of tapping in and replenishing when necessary.

So, do you see yourself having control issues, whether feeling like you need to have all control or that you don't have any? What can you do to find that happy medium of realistic expectations for yourself and those you love? Please pause here to reflect and write in your journal.

Change Fallacy

When you truly begin to do the work to discover who you are, you will begin to see the importance of being your authentic self. Of course, we want the people in our lives to show up in their authenticity as well. When you can perceive that both you and the individuals close to you are showing up as your authentic selves and not personas, you then naturally begin to pass judgment. You either like or don't like certain traits about them or yourself.

The fallacy of change will have you pressuring others to change because it becomes a contingency of your happiness. Even if the person makes the decision to change, resentment will undoubtedly set in and then you will have another set of problems.

You may have a family member, spouse, or friend who has a dependency on alcohol or pain medications. I have seen the pain of family members who are witnessing the medical complications of addiction time and time again. Often, they will make emphatic statements of how the patient has no choice and that they will change, they will get help, and they will develop better coping mechanisms to deal with life's challenges. I see and hear their desperation. Even if the patient is coerced into going to some type of rehabilitation program, it will be ineffective unless he or she makes the decision to seek help. This may be a time to speak the serenity prayer and ask for discernment on what you truly can change. This is typically your own actions or perceptions.

Fairness Fallacy

We all know that life is not designed to be fair. There are many clichés that speak to this: "only the good die young"; "the rich get richer and the poor get poorer." When we contemplate the "whys," it causes frustration. I am not talking about social injustices and discrimination, as these unfortunately are still seen today, often in disguise. However, the idea of unfairness sometimes boils down to personal preferences. If the less qualified coworker gets that promotion, what would be the most helpful response for you to have? Critically analyze factors that may have played into the decision besides what is on your resume. Look at it as an opportunity for growth. It may also be a time to reflect on the things that you truly want and desire, regardless of what appears to be an unfair blessing for your coworker. Tune in and spot any inkling of resentment and instead evaluate where you would like to be in your career and how you will get there. It may be time to pursue that entrepreneurial dream that has been deferred. The timing and circumstances in your life may be perfectly suited for you now!

Fallacy of Motives

As women, we sacrifice again and again. It is part of our makeup, as well as a trait that is encouraged because of our belief systems and cultures, which are more similar than one might suspect.

There may be an unconscious expectation, however, that you will get recognition and appreciation for the things that you do. You may also expect some reciprocation when you have a need. I know I often remind my youngest son of how blessed he is to have me and how grateful he ought to be! I have to be realistic about things. Cameron has the brain of a 13-year-old and has about ten more years before said brain will fully develop! There is no guarantee that I will feel appreciated then or now. When it comes to our relationships and goals for our lives,

the very acts that we engage in can be naturally rewarding. I certainly have had to catch myself focusing on the
wrong thing. I have the distinct memory of a time when
my actions to help someone had a paradoxical effect of my
being talked about, criticized, and unappreciated. It does
not take away from the joy that I felt doing the things that
I did or the benefits that I know the recipient received.
The rest is between her and God. So again, our happiness and sense of well-being is not contingent upon the
responses of others. The wellspring of joy is always inside us to provide the refreshing that we continually need.
You can feel the joy any time you decide and take actions
that will replenish it; i.e., take care of your mental, physical, and spiritual health.

CHAPTER 4

Negative Thought Processes

Filtering

How many times do you unconsciously use your brain as a mental strainer? You retain a negative outlook about something and let the positive go down the drain. Let's look at executive Sue. She is 30 years old and has recently been told by her primary physician that she is pre-diabetic and that losing at least 15 pounds will help prevent things from progressing. Sue has been very diligent about going to the gym three times a week and she even hired a personal trainer. She has been consistently losing two pounds over the last six weeks. It is week seven's weigh in and, much to her disappointment, she has not lost any weight, but has gained a pound. Sue's trainer has her lifting weights three times a week. He told her that muscle weighs more than fat and that she is toning up. Sue beats herself up and decides that she is just wasting her time and money. She sees this as a major setback and eats a bag of chips that night with a bowl of ice cream.

I wonder if you ever found yourself thinking and behaving like Sue. Unless she has a new mindset soon, she will continue to sabotage her efforts to improve her health and prevent disease. Instead of focusing on the progress that she has made, she focuses on something that she perceives as negative, even when her trainer had a positive interpretation of that one pound up on the scale. I know I am guilty of being overly critical of myself and now practice looking at the big picture when I catch myself discounting my blessings. This is called "reframing." What if in our scenario Sue's weight had remained the same? She could have said, "Well, I didn't lose any weight this week, but I am toning up and am only 3 lbs away from my goal!" I want you to take the next five minutes and see if you can think of a time in the past or present when you focused on a negative interpretation of something and discounted the positive. Once you write down the negative viewpoint, analyze the positive aspects about the situation and write these down. It is very important to take away the power of negative self-talk.

Personalization

Beth is 48 years old and the executive assistant at a marketing company. She works with a power team of women. Beth is known for her flamboyant style and brightly colored wardrobe. She can be very opinionated, but this does not cause any office drama. Everyone says, "That's just Beth." A group of five women from the office decided to have a girls' night when Beth just so happened to be out of town. She heard them talking about how much fun they had the Monday she returned. Her immediate thought was, "They must have decided to wait until I was not around to go out. They never agree with any of my proposals." Beth becomes distant and has a tough time focusing at work because she feels like the staff are talking behind her back. She is not sleeping well at night and gets a headache, which is unusual for her.

How often do you take things personally when there is no rational reason to do so? This is one negative thought pattern to watch out for if you find yourself thinking that the things people say or do are somehow directly related to you. It is a state of paranoia. If you recognize this as a dominant thought pattern, pause now to reflect. What past events in your life have had a negative impact on your self-image? Was there anything in your childhood? Are there vivid recollections of being taunted or put down? Some people can have such experiences, and it has the effect of making them fighting mad and eager to prove people wrong. Others may be more like I used to be and internalize the negativity, thereby increasing the odds of having self-fulfilling prophecies. In this case, Beth's reaction stems from her childhood when she was bullied. She was considered a nerd. She made significant efforts to improve her image, particularly when she went to college. The steps that she took only placed a band-aid on the old wounds that have not fully healed. She often resorts back to the hurt, vulnerable, defenseless young girl who wanted to be loved and accepted. What wounded areas do you still need help with nurturing to complete the healing process? Journaling and talk therapy may be helpful here. Focus on the value that you bring to not only the workplace but to the lives of those you love and care for. Of course, you are not perfect. When there is direct confrontation about who you are and what you are capable of, use it as an opportunity to grow. Resist being defensive. Ask yourself, what can I learn from this? What is life trying to teach me?

Catastrophizing

Amy is 50 years old and has been married to John for twenty years. They have a son, Sam, who is independent and doing well for himself. Amy is a teacher and enjoys working with her special-education students. John is a successful real estate agent. Amy has been supportive of her best friend, Lynn, whose husband recently left her for another woman.

Amy and John very rarely get into arguments but, one day, have a big blowup over a financial transaction that John made. The argument was not going anywhere, so John decided to leave the house to cool off. Amy was frantic and thought to herself that she should have never spoken to him the way that she did. She had a panic attack over the thought that he would not return and would probably fall into the arms of another woman just like Lynn's husband did. Her heart was racing, she was sweating, and she began to have chest pain.

In this scenario, Amy has allowed her thoughts to run wild, creating an extreme narrative. The runaway thoughts resulted in a physical reaction mimicking a heart attack. She is having an irrational thought process. When the thoughts popped into her mind, she got attached to them and began to have an emotional response leading to an unhealthy physical reaction.

We all can fall prey to some degree of catastrophizing, even if it does not have the extreme results as depicted here. You can take some steps to break the sequence the next time your imagination runs wild with you and causes undue stress. First, write down what happened. Be very objective without any commentary. This will consist of the irrefutable truths or the simple facts. Next, write down the conclusions that you have come to. Lastly, do you have the supporting evidence for your conclusions? In this scenario, would Amy's conclusion hold up in a court of law if she told the judge that her husband ran off to be with another woman that night? Do you see where

I am going? To re-shape your thinking, you must catch yourself in the act of jumping to conclusions and logically reason yourself out of them when necessary. You may have the type of personality where your vivid imagination can literally cause you to be sick. This typically stems from traumatic experiences from the past. Conditions like post-traumatic stress disorder can trigger such reactions. Please seek professional consultation from a psychiatrist if there is any concern.

Polarizing

Tanya is 38 years old and works as an assistant to the district attorney in her county. She is single and hates the fact that she is not married. Tanya grew up in a strict religious environment and has lived her life from the lens of dos and don'ts/rights and wrongs. She feels a tremendous amount of guilt when she has any temptation to have fun. She has only a small circle of friends and has not been out on a date in quite some time because she is looking for the perfect guy that she can feel comfortable with. She basically works and comes home to her cat Monday–Friday and is very lonely. Her high-school graduating class is having a reunion and several of her classmates have reached out to her on social media, encouraging her to participate. The reunion will be in Las Vegas, Nevada. Tanya declines the opportunity because she sees this as a trip to "SIN CITY." She reasons within herself that there is too much evil that she would encounter, and she can't handle it. She has been riddled with guilt over the fact that she has been drinking half a bottle of wine every night to help her sleep. She does not want her family to know about her drinking alcohol, as this was also prohibited growing up. She worries constantly about her parents finding out about her "secret sin." Of note, she recently had some blood work drawn as part of her annual checkup and was told by her doctor that her liver enzymes were elevated.

With a polarizing mindset, you see everything as black and white. There is no in between or room for error. You must be perfect. In Tanya's case, her belief system, ingrained in her from an early age, has shaped and framed her view of life as one of a sacrificial suffering and complete denial of anything deemed pleasurable or carnal. Life is not meant to be enjoyed and there is this fear of never measuring up to the standards that have been set for her. Tanya has never challenged the degree of strictness that she endured. She was an only child and her parents placed lofty expectations on her to conform to the rules. Her anxiety and guilt has resulted not only in a dysfunctional thinking pattern, but it has also resulted in addictive behavior that is starting to affect her physical health. What you see here is a positive feedback loop. It is positive in the sense that the pattern reinforces itself. Tanya feels lonely, has conflicting thoughts about what she can and can't do with her life, drinks to cope, then feels guilty. She continues to drink to numb the pain of loneliness and dull the perception of guilt. The cycle continues to repeat itself unless there is some intervention.

What limiting thoughts and beliefs might you have that are negatively impacting your health? I am not suggesting that you become a radical and denounce everything that you have been taught by those who had influence over you growing up. Instead, I am asking you to evaluate those areas that cause you unnecessary strife. What are the basic premises of these beliefs? How valid do you deem these basic premises to be based on your own critical thinking skills? If critical thinking was earlier discouraged by those in authority, there is room to sharpen this skill if you do the work. If you are alone and lonely, it is time to get comfortable with yourself and your thoughts. Don't be afraid of them or judge them. Be as objective as you can and resist blocking any thoughts that may be contrary to what you think you are supposed to hold true. Sit with this for a while and then give yourself permission to be enlightened and make healthy decisions about the direction you decide for your life.

Comparison

Rita is 55 years old. Everyone compliments her on how youthful she appears; most figure she is not a day past 40. Rita is a nurse and works at a primary-care clinic. After her divorce last year, she decides that "It's time to do me." Despite how beautiful everyone perceives her to be, Rita has major insecurities. She examines herself in the mirror every time she has a chance, looking for new furrows on her face. She has been getting routine Botox injections and has been saving up her money to have body contouring. Her magazine subscriptions are to Glamour and Vogue. She combs through the pages and says to herself, "If I could only look like that." Her appearance has become an obsession for her, and her adult children are concerned that she is going overboard due to her fear of aging. Rita has always had a competitive side. She started moonlighting at an urgent-care facility on the weekends so that she could get a new sports car. Her next-door neighbor just got a new red Corvette. Rita realizes that it is hard to "Keep up with the Joneses," but she is not going to let any dust settle under her for trying.

Do you find yourself chasing "IT"? It's the "I will be happy when _____." You can fill in the blank. Is it the man, the money, or fame? When you have this illusion, you are far from presence and chasing your tail. "It" does not exist. We all want to be happy. Can you choose happiness today? Remember our emotions? What we really want is a steady state. This is where we come back to that peaceful/accepting state regardless of what is or isn't happening in our lives. Rita here is seeking validation. It is not enough for her that she is generally liked and admired for her physical beauty. She is trying to fill that empty space. Do you have that space that seems to suck you in and deludes you into thinking that when "It" settles in, everything will be lovely and grand? When you attach your happiness to things, people, or events, you will continue to be disappointed. You see, even if "it" comes, after a while you will see that the hole is still there. Instead, start doing the work required to accept life as it unfolds and not attach anything that is outside of you to a perception of happiness. You already have it. It's a matter of making the mental shift that acknowledges that it is there to be experienced. Try to enjoy the simple things in life. Take a moment now to list at least five events in your lifetime that were simple or common and have brought you a great sense of satisfaction and a feeling of wholeness and purpose.

1.

2.

3.

4.

5.

Drama Roles

We live in the age where society sadly thrives on drama. As mentioned before, we see this with reality television and with the socio-political climate of the day. When it comes to your mental and physical health, a life of drama-filled relationships is also very detrimental. Drama can cause you to gain or lose weight, fall into a depression, and shorten your lifespan.

We all end up on the drama triangle from time to time. It's important, however, to recognize where you are and to make a conscious decision to shift when necessary. Where there is drama, it is important to determine your role. You may be in the victim mode. If you find yourself viewing things as always happening TO YOU, you will stay in drama. At times, you may be the hero, always trying to fix something or someone. Could you possibly be the villain, always looking for someone to blame (maybe yourself)? When you are in drama, you are below the line (see diagram page 60). Now let's describe the three roles:

1. Victim: In this role, you see yourself at the mercy of others. You believe that you are powerless, and you avoid taking responsibility. There is a declaration of pain and suffering. The victim can be described as the complainer and worry wart. The victim feels that life is not fair.

2. Hero: The hero reacts to pain by finding temporary means to avoid it. The expectation is that she will make herself and others feel better by her deeds. There is a tendency to fix problems and seek appreciation. Some common ways to drift from being present and in the moment, include gluttony, chemical addiction, over-promising, and care-taking. The hero is the protector, peacemaker, and an analyzer.

3. Villain: The villain blames the victim, hero, or self, believing that she is right and that it is not up for discussion. The drift from being above the line can be evidenced by dismissing, lecturing, and justifying. The villain is the critic, debater, and know it all.

Above and drama free

Below and on the drama

Triangle

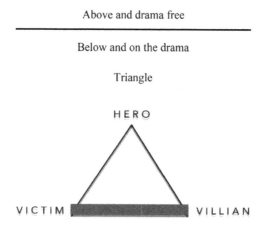

HERO

VICTIM   VILLIAN

Do you find yourself recycling old arguments with your spouse? Maybe you are the victim and he is the villain, while your mother is the hero or rescuer (serious drama). It is important when you feel conflict in your interactions to first locate your position. If you are in one of the three drama roles, you are below the line and will need to employ some techniques to shift above the line and get out of drama. Let's look at the roles again:

1. Victim: Life happens. We all have circumstances, such as a divorce, illness, loss of a job, and other unfortunate events. We have been victimized. This is different than being a "victim." The victim will continue to replay the past events and blame their unhappiness on their ex-spouse, boss, president, and next-door neighbor. It is essential to stop the pity party and ask yourself, "What is life trying to tell me?" If you view every experience as being perfectly orchestrated to help you learn and grow, you can get out of the victim role. With the example of a divorce, what role did you play in the suffering that you endured? What unresolved issues kept you in a codependent relationship where you neglected your needs and desires? You were getting something out of it, mostly in the form of self-punishment. Again, consider professional counseling to deal with the broken and wounded places in your heart.

2. Villain: When you are interacting with your spouse, or anyone for that matter, with whom you have a relationship, it is important to recognize any futile attempts at making others responsible for your happiness or your pain. Signs that you are in the role of the villain include yelling, blaming, and trying to make others feel guilty. When we blame others, we may be trying to avoid self-persecution. It is important to take it at face value when you are being called out as being the villain or persecutor. Try to replace statements that start with "you" to "I." For example, instead of "you always" try "I feel ... when you..." Sometimes, you need the objective view of a counselor.

3. Hero: As women, we are talented at nurturing and problem-solving for our loved ones. There is a pathologic version of this super woman and if this is you, it's time to retire your cape! The hero or rescuer is different than a helper. The helper is there if you need her and she waits to be called upon. Helpers also stop when the work is done, and they have altruistic motives. The hero, on the other hand, keeps on until she burns out. She wants to portray selflessness but really is looking for validation. You know you are in the hero role when you are asked to stop what you are doing, and you consider it a sign of ingratitude. Reflect and consider honestly if you have been or currently are in this role. Examine your true motives when you find yourself feeling a compulsion to help someone despite the drama that it creates or when you ignore the signs that they are trying to escape the victim role.

CHAPTER 6

Spiritual Health

I knew around age four that I would, one day, be a
doctor. It was in my spirit and was a gift from God.
There was no way that I could have come up with
the idea on my own. I had no role models or individuals
speaking into my life to create the desire. This was in
the 1960s, when there were less than 2% African-Amer-
ican female physicians in the US. As a child, there was
no apprehension about what I was going to do with my
life. It was not a goal because, at that age, I didn't know
what setting a goal meant! As I began to physically grow
and develop, I had many an external influence that was a
discouragement and distraction. Even falling in love got
in the way! There was the detour of marriage and working as a lab tech in the chemical industry. God always
had his purpose working for me despite the forces that at
first glance seemed to be working against me. God used
a broken spirit in the form of my husband to give me

gentle reminders of the task at hand. You see, we were kindred spirits in this area. He too wanted to become a physician but was divinely led to encourage me to pursue medicine. "When are you going to medical school?" was asked periodically. One day, after responding on multiple occasions, "You just don't go to medical school. You must be accepted," I picked up the phone to inquire about a review course to take the entrance exam. Mind you, I had been out of college for a decade. A plan was set in motion. I started taking some biology courses at the local college to refresh myself. One day, the cell biology professor said to me that it did not sound as though I was unfamiliar with the material, based on some of the questions that I had asked. He was informed that my objective was to go to medical school, but he wanted me to do some research in the lab with him and get my PhD. I thought it would be a valuable experience, so I worked with him for a semester, knowing all along that I was destined to become an MD. I was in my late 20s when I could have been already practicing medicine for a couple of years. It is advised that you apply to at least ten schools due to the competition. This is on the low end. My spirit, however, discerned that only one application was needed! This was for the University at Buffalo, in my hometown, where I had obtained my bachelor's degree ten years prior. And the rest is history.

I share this experience to serve as an example of how the spiritual realm operates. There is a spirit that dwells in you and is uniquely yours. No one else has or can have your spirit. Now, let me help you with your enlightenment. Have you ever awakened with a new thought or revelation and wondered where it came from? It is your spirit speaking to you. It is that experience where a thought is generated and your mind perceives it clearly. If you are very analytical as I am, you will try to figure out its relevance and determine if some action is needed. The spirit also discerns our thoughts. "For who knows a person's thoughts except their own spirit?" (1 Corinthians 2:11). So how spiritual are you? Some say, "I am spiritual but not religious." Being spiritual means that you practice balancing your inner needs with the rest of the world. There is a harmony that you strive for with yourself and others. You have the capacity to love and forgive. There is an effort toward finding fulfillment and meaning in life. You have an altruistic side and find joy in being of service to others. You are in the process of transcendence. As for me, I strive to have a balance of both the spiritual and what is considered religious. I am a Christian who has been striving to develop the closest relationship with God that I can. I understand that religious dogma and hypocrisy cause many to shun churches and religious organizations. Regardless of where you stand, what practices do you engage in that help your spiritual well-being? What are your core spiritual beliefs, and how true to them are you being? Which limiting beliefs do you possibly need to consider letting go of, based on the things that life has taught you—particularly the painful lessons? You may not have all the answers right now, but it is important to be open to revelation. When you can quiet the mind and stay still, your spiritual truths will encounter less resistance and competition. Some religions use the practice of fasting to help with personal decisions and direction in life. Many have reported a closer connection to God, which yields the benefits of more communication and communion, thereby granting peace. The spirit self is a divinely driven force that uses the mind to process and memorize things (something I obviously had to do a lot of with my medical training). It takes practicing mindfulness to take full advantage of what your spirit is trying to speak to you.

It is important that I also warn you about the dangers of letting others dictate your experience and awareness. Some may have good intentions but, in some instances, you may have unconsciously fallen prey to a certain level of brainwashing. Let me tell you that it does not take the degree of persuasion that Jim Jones had on his parishioners for you to act in ways that would go against your better judgment if you were to allow yourself to have judgment in the first place! As a young child, I found myself living in fear and guilt at a very young age. It may have been a part of my personality but a dogmatic spirit in the form of religious leadership reinforced my natural tendency to look to others for truth. I somehow concluded that they were more in tune with God and had a better understanding of those things pertinent to this life and in preparation for life beyond this realm. On the flip side, I can recall my early years in college, which started out at a Jesuit institution that required me to take numerous courses in philosophy. I really enjoyed learning about the philosophers' concepts on God and the world. I remember writing my essays and getting very enthralled as I could relate to their way of thinking, while at the same time formulating my own thoughts and ideas. This was encouraged and helped me ace these courses. Somehow, my life choices and influences in my early twenties began to take me away from that level of consciousness and I became trapped for over two decades! My situation and circumstances forced me into a new realm. I was divorced, and I now had a voice. It took some time for the voice to be acknowledged and discerned. God spoke through counselors who guided me back. Am I completely there? Well, not exactly. I am getting friendly reminders and encouragement along the way that I am on the right path.

I no longer live in black and white. Yes, there are fundamental truths and beliefs that I hold and freely share in the spirit of love. The problem with this world, however, both secular and religious, is that we are dealing with egos and the inherent desire to always be right! If we could shift our mindset to look at ourselves, have an open heart, practice loving ourselves, forgiving ourselves, I believe we can then share these gifts with others. We will live with more internal peace and feel less inclined to point the finger at others and place them under the microscope.

I am from Western New York, where there are more overcast days than not. I did not realize how my mood was affected until I moved south. Regardless of the temperature, I thrive on sunshine. My spirit tells my mind to go on hiking excursions. I move into action, my body gets the exercise that it needs, and my brain releases euphoric hormones that feed my mind. I hope you see the interconnection here. Set aside some time this week to ask your spirit what messages are being dampened by the cares of this life, or more specifically YOUR LIFE. It takes a conscious effort and plan. As an example, my morning consisted of prayer, meditation, praise, and worship. The result has been renewal, inspiration, and motivation to get my message to you.

Your Needs, My Needs...Really, Our Needs

Before we delve into creating your personal health and wellness plan, I would like for you to consider some universal human needs that we all have. I will cover a few here. First, we have a subsistence need. This deals with having the minimum resources to support yourself. Of course, you want to live in abundance, but that is a relative concept. It requires that you can separate your basic needs from what you desire or want. Now, I hope that I can inspire you to think, dream, and act big, but having a realistic idea of what you need in the physical realm that you live in will go a long way. From a physical perspective, you need food, shelter, and clothing. It's time to take a walk when you can at your home (after you have been grocery shopping). Take an inventory of what you have in your cupboards and refrigerator. Then, walk through your bedroom closet and open your dressers. Pause, look, and become aware of all the four-walled rooms in your home. I venture to guess that you have more than just a minimal number of physical things that you need to survive and can probably share with others, even after your household family members' needs are accounted for. Now, let's look at your financial resources. List your monthly input from all sources in one column and your monthly expenses in the next. Then take a red pen and cross out the items in your expense column that can be classified as a luxury or can be identified as something that you enjoy but is not one of the basic needs. Lastly, if you work, calculate the total hours worked per week and note your net take-home income. Are you working two jobs or overtime? If the answer is yes, write down what the cost is to your mental and physical health. Are the extra hours encroaching on the number of hours you spend sleeping at night or the time that you can use to exercise and prepare healthy meals? If the answer is yes, re-examine your financial minimum and determine how many of the red lines need to now be whited out. Your expense can become your surplus. No price tag can be placed on your health, which, if not properly maintained, will make all of the arduous work a vain endeavor.

As women, we are typically viewed as the affectionate ones. Not every woman, however, expresses affection for spouse, family, or friends the same way. Strictly speaking, affection is a feeling of fondness or tenderness for a person. Research has shown that experiencing affection physically (non-sexual) is right up there with food, water, and rest as a basic need. If a person desires having affection expressed in a physical way, and is not getting it, there can be a sense of "skin hunger," which can affect their health negatively. There is a higher incidence of loneliness, depression, and anxiety. Physical touch increases hormones that make you feel happy, decreases levels of stress hormones, and lowers blood pressure. I came from a family of huggers. There have been times when friends have commented on how much they like my bear hugs! You can prescribe yourself a daily hug to be given to your spouse, child, or other loved one before you start your day. It can give you a sense of wellness that lasts throughout the day! Sometimes, the ones we love and care for just need a hug. Being willing to participate and give/receive can help nurture bonding. You may, however, be one who experiences affection with words that affirm your connection. Share this with your spouse/mate and give positive reinforcement when he does speak your love language this way.

Autonomy is another need that we all have and, at times, can be thwarted by outside forces. Having a good sense of autonomy means that you don't feel pressured or coerced into believing and doing things in a way that may not work for you. At the same time, you have an open mind and can see things from someone else's perspective without passing judgment. A lack of autonomy can cause unhealthy stress and frustration. Is there an area in your life where not experiencing enough autonomy is negatively affecting your mental health? What can you do to start walking in your own truth and take the power back? This can be challenging in the workplace, depending on the nature of what you do. Sometimes the frustration of not having enough autonomy may spark an interest in exploring other options, including that entrepreneurial spirit to step out on your own. Going out on a limb may be the best thing because of the rewarding fruit awaiting you.

While we all need to be able to walk in our self-directed path, at the same time we have a need to belong and have a sense of community. You want to feel heard and appreciated. This need for a sense of belonging crosses all cultures. We all need a minimal quantity of high quality social interactions. When you feel accepted and welcomed, there is a sense of calm and happiness versus anxiety, jealousy, and depression when you don't. How would you rate your overall sense of connectedness? Do you have common purpose with others, be it in a church community, sorority, or social club? If not, take time to write a list of organizations or groups that you want to become a part of or experience for the sheer pleasure of it. I felt connected with a group of complete strangers while hiking today. As usual, the experience was enhanced by the Law of Attraction. I met like-minded people willing to share a part of their lives with me on levels that were not by happenstance.

Lastly, there is a need that you probably don't give conscious thought to, but which is at the root of certain goals. Whether you are pushing yourself from engaging in no physical activity to doing a triathlon or searching for meaning in life, you are trying to transcend. In this process, you end up existing or having experiences beyond the normal. There are key components with spiritual transcendence. There is a certain appreciation of beauty that you see in what on the surface is not extraordinary. You develop a sense of gratitude for life and find ways to express it. There is an awareness of a higher purpose, and you begin to see where you fit in, what your role is. You are full of hope and have a greater sense of humor. If you have never seen yourself in a state of transcendence, it is my prayer that you have been sparked to be creative as you are designing your life moving forward. Your transcendent state is akin to the "ah-ha" moments that are full of peace, tranquility, and satisfaction.

CHAPTER 7

Personal Health and Wellness Plan

Now that you have gained some enlightenment sur-
rounding your mental and spiritual health needs, it is
time to take everything that has been considered up to
this point and begin working on definitive goals for your
growth and healing. This outline should be used for your
physical health goals as well. Before you can create your
health and wellness plan, it is important to identify what
your core values are. Your personality, upbringing, and
life experiences shape your core values; your goals should
reflect them.

Step 1. List ten of your core values. As an example,
I value my relationship with God, quality family time,
physical activity, and good health. Sometimes, core values change as we live and go through some things. Critically analyze your list and see if each value still holds true

for you. Don't use your behavior as a barometer though. We don't always behave the way our core values would otherwise dictate.

1.

2.

3.

4.

5.

6.

7.

8.

9.

10.

Step 2. Using your core values, list one SMART goal for each area of health. Make sure the goal is SPECIFIC, MEASURABLE, ACHIEVEABLE, REALISTIC, and TIME-BOUND:

    a.   Mental-Health Goal

b. Physical-Health Goal

c. Spiritual-Health Goal

Step 3. Use a planner to pencil in your daily ACTIVI-TIES that will help you start the process of achieving optimal health and wellness.

Step 4. Create a vision board, use written positive affirmations, share your journey with a close friend for accountability, and inspire!

Your health and wellness plan will evolve with time because you are evolving. You should make weekly assessments and necessary adjustments to the goals that you have. You will be inspired to use whatever resources necessary to accomplish them, including your primary physician, other healthcare providers, therapists, and personal trainers as needed.

We have covered a large territory. I hope that my sharing about my life experiences, from my professional medical eyes, coupled with the shared experience of womanhood, has helped you see the connection between your mental, spiritual, and physical health.

We started with the concept of practicing mindfulness, followed by gaining a deeper appreciation of your thoughts and emotions. You now see that emotions are not your enemy nor the pilot of your flight.

You now have insight into some of the common psychological barriers to maintaining healthy relationships and are committed to practicing mind shifting and staying out of drama. You are more than a conqueror! Healthy living for you, my sister, is more than meets the mind. It is fueled by the daily renewal and transformation of YOUR mind.

From My Heart to Yours...

You are the author of your life story as you nurture your mental, spiritual, and physical essence. Regardless of prior chapters in the story of your life, I have every confidence that you are more than capable of writing new ones and creating the best version of yourself.

Instead of viewing life's challenges and disappointments in a negative light, look at how everything has given you new perspective and empowerment to move forward with optimism, joy, and peace.

Promise to practice self-compassion. Even your mistakes and failures have their place in your bright future. No one who is successful has escaped them. What is your definition of success? It's not what others have defined for you, but rather a joining of your spirit to what has been pre-ordained for you. God saw my unformed body, all the days ordained for me were written in His book before one of them came to be... Psalm 137:16. I believe this with and for you!

You may feel as if you are spinning your wheels. Maybe it's time for a new set of wheels that have the traction needed to roll and move despite the condition of the road. It can be slippery with ice and sometimes warped by sweltering heat! But we must put the car in gear and move. Forget about the reverse mode once you have been redirected and are heading in the right direction. Ask God to give you the guidance, the road map to your destiny, and guess what? He will send you confirmation along the way on how you are doing.

Trust and believe that the world is on your side. When you see every experience, disappointment, trial, and tribulation as your ally, perfectly designed to teach you, you will use the lessons as fuel for executing your mission.

Nurturing your mind, body, and soul is key for your efficient use of the blessing of time that we all have each waking day and with each breath that we take.

When you begin to follow your heart and live your dreams, you are creating your own happiness. Dream big! God did not create you for smallness. You don't have to operate in your own strength, but take comfort in knowing that strength is given to you. That's what all the heartache and challenge has been about all along.

What gets you excited and passionate at the mere thought of it? This is what matters to you most. Pray that it is in alignment with spiritual goodness and for the insight to move into action in the healthiest fashion.

You are the real thing, perfect in all your flaws, which are really God's stamp of uniqueness. Strength and dignity are your clothing. Pray for discernment to use your gifts wisely. Embrace your journey and never stop learning.

Remember to laugh out loud and enjoy the simple things in life. Awaken your senses to nature, which has been designed for your enjoyment and delight.

Remember that there is a time for every purpose under heaven. You are like the olive tree and have gone through many a pruning season. This process is never enjoyable, but it is required for fruit-bearing and harvesting.

You and I were destined to converge on and engage in this spiritual communication. I pray that you have been blessed by it to be a blessing to others. Look out for your fellow sister along the way. You have been down a similar path and can offer her some tools to help her trudge through the oftentimes rocky, steep, muddy jungle with faith that the clear path is not far-off.

About the Author

Dr. Indie Jones is a board certified internist who has treated thousands of women and men for acute disease processes in the hospital setting in and around Atlanta, Georgia. Her passion however, is helping women become the champions of their mental, physical, and spiritual health.

For more information regarding her on-line e-books, e-courses, and seminars, visit mindfulhealth4women.com.

To book for speaking engagements, send an e-mail request to docindie@mindfulhealth4women.com

Made in the USA
Monee, IL
24 April 2022

95317740R00056